Early one morning a roadrunner was sitting on top of a prickly pear cactus. From his perch he could see for miles across the hot Arizona desert. To the right he saw footprints in the dry sand. To the left he saw many broken brambles of chaparral.

On the ground the roadrunner saw a partially eaten prickly pear fruit. "Ha–ha!" he said.
"A javelina's been here."

Just then a lizard passed by and said,
"What did you say?"

The roadrunner smiled, saying,
"Have you seen a javelina?"

"No," said the lizard,
"I haven't seen a javelina.
What does it look like?"

The roadrunner replied,
> *A javelina has sharp tusks*
> *And a long, hairy snout,*
> *For digging insects, snakes,*
> *And lizards out!*

"Oh my, I'm one of those creatures!" said the lizard. "What shall I do if I see one?"

The roadrunner answered,
> *I would find a safe place to stay*
> *Until the javelina goes away.*

Just then a sidewinder slithered by,
and the roadrunner asked the snake,
"Have you seen a javelina?"

The snake replied,
"No, I haven't seen a javelina.
Where does it hide?"

The roadrunner said,
    A javelina sleeps
    Under bushes at night.
    There it is safe,
    Hidden far out of sight.

"Oh my, that is where I sleep at night!" the snake said. "What shall I do if I see one?"

The roadrunner said,
> I would find a safe place to stay
> Until the javelina goes away.

Just then a tarantula crept by.
The roadrunner said to the tarantula,
"Have you seen a javelina?"

The tarantula replied,
"No, I haven't seen a javelina.
Is it a good runner?"

The roadrunner said,
    A javelina runs fast.
    He's built low to the ground,
    So he sees all the little things
    Crawling around.

"Oh my, I'm always crawling around here!" the tarantula said. "What shall I do if I see one?"

The roadrunner said,
> *I would find a safe place to stay*
> *Until the javelina goes away.*

By noon the desert was so hot
that even the saguaro cactus seemed to sag.
The wavy lines of heat wiggled across
the desert landscape.

The armadillos were rolled up
into little sweat balls.

The desert tortoises were
complaining of prickly heat.

The scorpions were
cracking in their armor.

The prickly pears began
to pop in the heat.

The roadrunner was stretched out, taking
a little nap in the shade of some boulders.
He was sleeping so soundly that
he didn't even hear the javelina
as it came into the clearing
and started digging around
for moist things to eat.
The javelina filled up first
on the prickly pear,
then it spied the roadrunner
sleeping, and thought to itself,

*I know I could never
Run faster than he could,
But a roadrunner snack
Would certainly taste good.*

12

The javelina was just about to gore the little roadrunner with its sharp tusks when the roadrunner woke up.

"What a miserable way to go–" thought the roadrunner, "a bird shish kebab!" And he cried out,
    Oh my! Javelina, don't you dare!
    Don't eat me up like a prickly pear!
    Come on, Javelina, don't eat me.
    I'd taste worse than a Joshua tree.

The javelina stopped in its tracks.
It was surprised that anyone
would talk to it at all.
All the creatures of the desert
hid away whenever
it came around.

The roadrunner was
proud of his cleverness.
He puffed himself up.
The javelina couldn't
help but notice that
the roadrunner looked
plump and tasty.
It bent over the
roadrunner and,
with the nicest smile
it could muster, said...

*Dear Roadrunner,
You're the best of the bunch,
But I'm afraid you're still
Going to be my lunch!*

And so it was in the hot desert sun,
that finally the story was over and done.

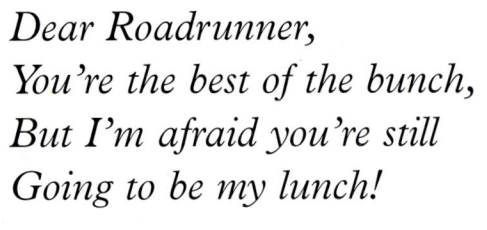